John C.

Portraits and Sketches of the Lives of All the Candidates for

the Presidency

and Vice-Presidency, for 1860 - comprising eight portraits engraved on

steel, facts in the life of each

John C. Buttre

Portraits and Sketches of the Lives of All the Candidates for the Presidency
*and Vice-Presidency, for 1860 - comprising eight portraits engraved on steel, facts
in the life of each*

ISBN/EAN: 9783337848224

Printed in Europe, USA, Canada, Australia, Japan

Cover: Foto ©Andreas Hilbeck / pixelio.de

More available books at **www.hansebooks.com**

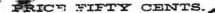
PORTRAITS

AND

SKETCHES OF THE LIVES

OF

All the Candidates

FOR THE

PRESIDENCY AND VICE-PRESIDENCY,

FOR 1860.

COMPRISING

PORTRAITS ENGRAVED ON STEEL, FACTS IN THE LIFE OF EACH,
THE FOUR PLATFORMS, THE CINCINNATI PLATFORM,

AND

TITUTION OF THE UNITED STATES.

STREET.

PORTRAITS

AND

SKETCHES OF THE LIVES

OF

All the Candidates

FOR THE

PRESIDENCY AND VICE-PRESIDENCY,

FOR 1860.

COMPRISING

EIGHT PORTRAITS ENGRAVED ON STEEL, FACTS IN THE LIFE OF EACH,
THE FOUR PLATFORMS, THE CINCINNATI PLATFORM,

AND

THE CONSTITUTION OF THE UNITED STATES.

―――・・◆・・◆――

New-York:

J. C. BUTTRE, 48 FRANKLIN STREET.

――

1860.

ABRAHAM LINCOLN,

OF ILLINOIS.

———◆◆———

ABRAHAM LINCOLN was born in Hardin county, Kentucky, February 12, 1809, and is now 51 years old. His parents were born in Virginia, and were of very moderate circumstances. His paternal grandfather, Abraham Lincoln, emigrated from Rockingham county, Va., to Kentucky, about 1781, '82, where, a year or two later, he was killed by Indians. His ancestors, who were respectable members of the Society of Friends, went to Virginia from Berks county, Pennsylvania. Thomas, the father of the present subject, by the early death of his father, and very narrow circumstances of his mother, even in childhood, was a wandering, laboring boy, and grew up literally without education. He married Nancy Hanks, mother of the present subject, in 1806. The family removed from Kentucky to Spencer county, in Indiana, in the autumn of 1816, Abraham being then in his eighth year.

Mr. Lincoln received a limited education. Probably six months in all, of the rudest sort of schooling, comprehends the whole of his technical education. He was in turn a farm laborer, a common workman in a saw-mill, and a boatman on the Wabash and Mississippi rivers. Thus hard work and plenty of it, the rugged experiences of aspiring poverty, the wild sports and rude games of a newly and thinly peopled forest region—the education born of the log-cabin, the rifle, the axe, and the plough, combined with the reflections of an original and vigorous mind, eager in the pursuit of knowledge by every available means, and developing a character of equal resource and firmness, made him the man he has since proved himself.

At twenty-one he pushed further west into Illinois, which has for the last thirty years been his home, living always near, and, for some years past, in Springfield, the State Capital. He worked on a farm, as a hired man, his first year in Illinois ; the next year he was a clerk in a store ; then volunteered for the Black-Hawk war, and was chosen a captain by his company ; the next year he was an unsuccessful candidate for the Legislature ; he was chosen the next, and served four sessions with eminent usefulness and steadily increasing reputation ; studied law, meantime, and took his place at the bar ; was early recognized as a most effective and convincing advocate, before the people, of Whig principles and the Protective policy, and of their illustrious embodiment, Henry Clay ; was a Whig candidate for Elector in nearly or quite every Presidential contest from 1836 to 1852, inclusive ; was chosen to the Thirtieth Congress, from the Central District of Illinois, in 1846, and served to its close, but was not a candidate for re-election ; and in 1849, measurably withdrew from politics and devoted himself to the practice of his profession until the Nebraska Bill, of 1854, called him again into the political arena. He was the candidate of the Whigs for United States Senator before the Legislature chosen that year ; but they were not a majority of the body ; so he declined, and urged his friends to support Judge Trumbull, the candidate of the anti-Nebraska Democrats, who was thus elected.

In the gallant and memorable Presidential contest of 1856, Mr. Lincoln's name headed the Fremont Electoral Ticket of Illinois. In 1858, he was unanimously designated by the Republican State Convention to succeed Mr. Douglas in the Senate ; and thereupon canvassed the State against Mr. Douglas, with an ability in which logic, art, eloquence, and thorough good-nature were alike conspicuous, and which gave him a national reputation. Mr. Douglas secured a predominance in the Legislature and was elected, though Mr. Lincoln had the larger popular vote.

In personal appearance Mr. Lincoln is long, lean, and wiry. In motion he has a great deal of the elasticity and awkwardness which indicate the rough training of his early life. His face is genial looking. His hair is dark, tinged with gray, a good forehead, small eyes, a long nose, and a large mouth, which is probably the most expressive feature of his face. His height is six feet three inches. He is a man of the People, raised by his own genius and integrity from the humblest to the highest position, having made himself an honored name, as a lawyer, an advocate, a popular orator, a statesman, and a man.

HANNIBAL HAMLIN,

OF MAINE.

———————

HANNIBAL HAMLIN was born in Paris, Oxford county, Maine, August 27th, 1809, and is now in the fifty-first year of his age. He is by profession a lawyer, but for the last twenty-four years has spent most of the time in political life. From 1836 to 1840, he was a member of the legislature of Maine, and for three of those years was Speaker of its House of Representatives. In 1843 he was elected a member of Congress, and re-elected for the following term. In 1847 he was again a member of the House of Representatives of the State Legislature. He was elected to the United States Senate, May 26th, 1848, for four years, to fill a vacancy occasioned by the death of John Fairfield. He was re-elected for the full term in the same body, July 25th, 1851, and elected Governor of Maine, January 7th, 1857, resigning his seat in the Senate, and being inaugurated Governor the same day. On the 16th of the same month he was again elected to the United States Senate, for six years, which office he accepted, and resigned the office of Governor.

He is now a United States Senator from Maine, and a member of the Committee on Commerce and on the District of Columbia. This record is an evidence of the confidence with which he has always been regarded by his fellow-citizens in Maine.

Up to the time of the passage of the Kansas-Nebraska bill, in 1854, Mr. Hamlin was a member of the Democratic party. That act he regarded as a proof that the party with which he had been all his life connected, no longer deserved the name of democratic, and was treacherous to the principles he had so long cherished. He changed his politics, in a speech in the Senate, on the Nebraska bill, and thenceforward gave his support to the Republican party, of which he has ever since continued a faithful and distinguished leader.

Mr. Hamlin is a man of dignified presence, of solid abilities, of unflinching integrity, and great executive talent.

REPUBLICAN PLATFORM,

PUT FORTH AT CHICAGO, MAY 18, 1860.

———•———

Resolved, That we, the delegated representatives of the Republican Electors of the United States, in convention assembled, in the discharge of the duty we owe to our constituents and our country, unite in the following declarations:

1. That the history of the nation, during the last four years, has fully established the propriety and necessity of the organization and perpetuation of the Republican party, and that the causes which called it into existence are permanent in their nature, and now, more than ever before, demand its peaceful and constitutional triumph.

2. That the maintenance of the principles promulgated in the Declaration of Independence, and embodied in the Federal Constitution, is essential to the preservation of our republican institutions; that the Federal Constitution, the rights of the States, and the Union of the States, must and shall be preserved; and that we reassert "these truths to be self-evident, that all men are created equal; that they are endowed by their Creator with certain inalienable rights; that among these are life, liberty, and the pursuit of happiness. That to secure these rights, governments are instituted among men, deriving their just powers from the consent of the governed."

3. That to the Union of the States this nation owes its unprecedented increase in population; its surprising development of material resources; its rapid augmentation of wealth; its happiness at home and its honor abroad; and we hold in abhorrence all schemes for disunion, come from whatever source they may; and we congratulate the country that no Republican member of Congress has uttered or countenanced a threat of disunion, so often made by Democratic members of Congress without rebuke, and with applause from their political associates; and we denounce those threats of disunion, in case of a popular overthrow of their ascendency, as denying the vital principles of a free government, and as an avowal of contemplated treason, which it is the imperative duty of an indignant people strongly to rebuke and forever silence.

4. That the maintenance inviolate of the rights of the States, and especially the right of each State to order and control its own domestic institutions according to its own judgment exclusively, is

essential to that balance of power on which the perfection and endurance of our political faith depends ; and we denounce the lawless invasion, by armed force, of any State or Territory, no matter under what pretext, as among the gravest of crimes.

5. That the present Democratic Administration has far exceeded our worst apprehensions in its measureless subserviency to the exactions of a sectional interest, as is especially evident in its desperate exertions to force the infamous Lecompton Constitution upon the protesting people of Kansas—in construing the personal relation between master and servant to involve an unqualified property in persons—in its attempted enforcement everywhere, on land and sea, through the intervention of Congress and the Federal Courts, of the extreme pretensions of a purely local interest, and in its general and unvarying abuse of the power intrusted to it by a confiding people.

6. That the people justly view with alarm the reckless extravagance which pervades every department of the Federal Government ; that a return to rigid economy and accountability is indispensable to arrest the system of plunder of the public treasury by favored partisans ; while the recent startling developments of fraud and corruption at the Federal metropolis show that an entire change of administration is imperatively demanded.

7. That the new dogma, that the Constitution, of its own force, carries slavery into any or all the Territories of the United States, is a dangerous political heresy, at variance with the explicit provisions of that instrument itself, with contemporaneous exposition, and with legislative and judicial precedent, is revolutionary in its tendency and subversive of the peace and harmony of the country.

8. That the normal condition of all the territory of the United States is that of freedom ; that as our republican fathers, when they abolished slavery in all our national territory, ordained that no person should be deprived of life, liberty, or property, without due process of law, it becomes our duty, by legislation, whenever such legislation is necessary, to maintain this provision of the Constitution against all attempts to violate it ; and we deny the authority of Congress, of a Territorial Legislature, or of any individuals, to give legal existence to slavery in any Territory of the United States.

9. That we brand the recent re-opening of the African slave-trade, under the cover of our national flag, aided by perversions of judicial power, as a crime against humanity, a burning shame to our country and age ; and we call upon Congress to take prompt and efficient measures for the total and final suppression of that execrable traffic.

10. That in their recent vetoes, by their Federal Governors, of the acts of the Legislatures of Kansas and Nebraska, prohibiting slavery in those Territories, we find a practical illustration of the boasted Democratic principle of non-intervention and popular sovereignty, embodied in the Kansas and Nebraska bill, and a demonstration of the deception and fraud involved therein.

11. That Kansas should, of right, be immediately admitted as a

State, under the constitution recently formed and adopted by her people, and accepted by the House of Representatives.

12. That while providing revenue for the support of the General Government by duties upon imposts, sound policy requires such an adjustment of these imposts as to encourage the development of the industrial interests of the whole country; and we commend that policy of national exchanges which secures to the working men liberal wages, to agriculture remunerating prices, to mechanics and manufacturers an adequate reward for their skill, labor, and enterprise, and to the nation commercial prosperity and independence.

13. That we protest against any sale or alienation to others of the public lands held by actual settlers, and against any view of the free homestead policy which regards the settlers as paupers or supplicants for public bounty; and we demand the passage by Congress of the complete and satisfactory homestead measure which has already passed the House.

14. That the Republican party is opposed to any change in our naturalization laws, or any State legislation by which the rights of citizenship hitherto accorded to immigrants from foreign lands shall be abridged or impaired; and in favor of giving a full and efficient protection to the rights of all classes of citizens, whether native or naturalized, both at home and abroad.

15. That appropriations by Congress for river and harbor improvements, of a national character, required for the accommodation and security of an existing commerce, are authorized by the Constitution, and justified by an obligation of the government to protect the lives and property of its citizens.

16. That a railroad to the Pacific ocean is imperatively demanded by the interests of the whole country; that the Federal Government ought to render immediate and efficient aid in its construction, and that as preliminary thereto, a daily overland mail should be promptly established.

17. Finally, having thus set forth our distinctive principles and views, we invite the co-operation of all citizens, however differing on other questions, who substantially agree with us, in their affirmance and support.

to vote for a resolution approving that measure. This refusal was one of the causes which led to the subsequent breach between himself and President Jackson and the Democratic party, and finally to his co-operation with the Whigs. This change of party relations was much accelerated by his election to the speakership of the House of Representatives, in 1834.

In June of that year Mr. Stevenson resigned the chair upon being nominated minister to Great Britain, and Mr. Bell was elected to succeed him. Mr. Bell was supported by the Whigs and a portion of the Democratic party who were opposed to the intended nomination of Martin Van Buren as successor to General Jackson. The principal ground of Mr. Bell's opposition to Mr. Van Buren was his strong disapproval of the system of removals from subordinate offices for political reasons. The final separation between Mr. Bell and Gen. Jackson took place in 1835, when Mr. Bell declared himself in favor of Judge White for the Presidency, in opposition to Mr. Van Buren. Judge White carried the State by a large majority, and Mr. Bell was re-elected to Congress. An impulse was given to the political character of Tennessee, which arrayed in its opposition to the Democracy during the four succeeding Presidential elections, 1840–'44–'48–'52.

When the reception of petitions for the abolition of slavery in the District of Columbia was agitated in the House of Representatives, in 1836, Mr. Bell alone, of the Tennessee delegation, favored their reception. Subsequently, in 1838, when Atherton's resolutions were introduced, proposing to receive and lay these petitions on the table, he maintained his consistency by voting in the negative.

General Harrison, when elected President, invited Mr. Bell to enter his Cabinet as Secretary of War, a position which he resigned after Mr. Tyler became President. He was then tendered a seat in the Senate, but declined in favor of Mr. Foster. In 1847 he was elected, and in 1853 re-elected, a United States Senator from Tennessee; and his course in favor of the compromise measures, the internal improvement bills, the increase of our steam navy, a Pacific railroad, agricultural colleges, and other similar measures, was as marked as was his opposition to the Nebraska Bill, the Lecompton Constitution, extravagant expenditures, and threats of disunion.

Since his retirement from public life he has resided at his home in Nashville, where his accomplished wife and daughters are ever ready to join him in extending genuine Tennessee hospitality to their numerous friends.

EDWARD EVERETT,

OF MASSACHUSETTS.

————•——

Mr Everett was born at Dorchester, Massachusetts, in 1794. The son of a New-England clergyman, he was educated with the care which such a father was likely to bestow on his son. So precocious was he, that at thirteen he matriculated at Harvard, and graduated with honors four years later. His aptitude as a linguist was so notorious that the ruling powers of Harvard College kept their eye on him ; and soon after he left the University, before he was twenty-one, he was offered the professorship of Greek, with the condition that, if he accepted it, he must spend some years in European travel, in order to fit himself for his duties.

In 1819, Mr. Everett entered upon the discharge of his duties as Professor of Greek ; and shortly afterward, the editorship of the *North American Review* falling vacant, he assumed charge of that journal, and raised it to high rank in literature.

In 1824, when Mr. Everett was thirty years of age, he began, simultaneously, his career as a politician and as an orator. An oration which he delivered in presence of the venerable Lafayette, in that year, attracted universal attention to his extraordinary powers ; and from that time forth he became one of the leading orators of the country. In the same year he was sent to Congress from Middlesex. In the House he was chiefly noted for his industrious habits and vast learning. He was an invaluable man on committees. On all debates of importance his voice was heard ; but he never sought to make speeches for the sake of hearing his own voice. What he said was brief and to the point. Strangers, especially from New-England, frequently thronged the House when he was to speak, in the expectation of hearing a grand oration, but they were generally disappointed. Mr. Everett never made a show of oratory in the House.

After ten years arduous labor in Congress, Mr. Everett was elected Governor of Massachusetts, which office he filled for four consecutive years.   In 1839 he was again a candidate, but was defeated by one vote out of over one hundred thousand cast.   This defeat happily left him free to accept the mission to England which was tendered to him by the administration of General Harrison, in 1841.

He was absent for four years, during which time he won golden opinions from persons of every class in England.   Few American statesmen stand as high as Edward Everett in the British judgment at the present time. He was described by an Englishman as " a man firm and unbending as a rock on important questions, yet so conciliatory as to lead every one to suppose that he was ready to yield every point in dispute : keen, and close in argument, stuffed full of facts, and as obstinate a Yankee as you could meet with in a month's journey in New-England."

On his return to this country he assumed the Presidentship of his old University at Cambridge. A fortunate marriage had happily placed him beyond the necessity of daily labor for a livelihood. He was enabled to indulge to his heart's content in the studies dear to him, and which are life's best solace.

Accident disturbed his pleasing labors. On the death of Daniel Webster, he was unexpectedly called, by President Fillmore, to fill a leading office in the Cabinet—the Secretaryship of State.   He abandoned his library, and betook himself to the drudgery of official life with as much cheerfulness as he had displayed when his first public honors burst upon him. His most important public act—his letter on the Cuba question—was indited and published after his resignation of office ; but the character of the man gave it importance ; and there is reason to believe that it was not without influence on the minds of the leading statesmen in England.   A subsequent brief senatorial career justified the expectations which had been entertained of Mr. Everett. He played the part of a philosopher and a sage, and held himself aloof from the petty squabbles of politicians.

His subsequent career has been tranquil.   His oration on charity ; his oration on Washington, the profits of which are destined for the Washington Monument, and which has done more for that structure than all the private contributions of the public put together ; his oration on Astronomy, at the opening of the Albany Geological Hall, in August, 1856, are masterpieces of eloquence, which will live for centuries after Burke, and Sheridan, and Patrick Henry, and will be learned by boys in schools in ages far hidden in the future.

UNION PLATFORM,

PUT FORTH AT BALTIMORE, MAY 10TH, 1860.

———•———

Whereas, Experience has demonstrated that platforms adopted by the partisan conventions of the country have had the effect to mislead and deceive the people, and, at the same time, to widen the political divisions of the country, by the creation and encouragement of geographical and sectional parties, therefore,

Resolved, That it is both the part of patriotism and of duty to recognize no political principles other than the Constitution of the country, the Union of the States, and the enforcement of the laws; and, as the representatives of the Constitutional Union men of the country, in National Convention assembled, we here pledge ourselves to maintain, protect, and defend, separately and unitedly, these great principles of public liberty and national safety, against all the enemies at home and abroad; believing, thereby, that peace may once more be restored to the country, the just rights of the people and of the States re-stablished, and the government again placed in that condition of justice, fraternity. and equality which, under the example and Constitution of our fathers, has solemnly bound every citizen of the United States to maintain a more perfect union, establish justice, secure domestic tranquillity, provide for the common defence, promote the general welfare, and secure the blessings of liberty to ourselves and our posterity.

STEPHEN A. DOUGLAS,

OF ILLINOIS.

———◆———

STEPHEN A. DOUGLAS was born at Brandon, Rutland county, Vermont, 23d of April, 1813. He is a descendant of the great Scotch family of the same name. Dr. Stephen A. Douglas, the father of the statesman of the present day, in July, 1813, while holding Stephen in his arms, died suddenly of disease of the heart.

His earlier days were spent with his mother and sister upon a farm, but his mother being left in destitute circumstances, he entered a cabinet shop at Middlebury, in his native State, for the purpose of learning the trade. After remaining there for several months, he returned to Brandon, where he continued for a year at the same calling, but his health obliged him to abandon it, and he became a student in the academy. His mother having married a second time, he followed her to Canandaigua, in the State of New-York. Here he pursued the study of the law until his removal to Cleveland, Ohio, in 1813. From Cleveland, he went still farther west, and finally settled in Jacksonville, Illinois. He was first employed as clerk to an auctioneer, and afterward kept school, devoting all the time he could spare to the study of the law.

In March, 1834, still lacking one month of being twenty-one years old, he was admitted to the bar by the Supreme Court, and opened a law office in Jacksonville. He soon became known as an ardent Democrat, and at the meeting of the next Legislature was elected Attorney-General of the State. Mr. Douglas was elected and took his seat in the Legislature in the winter of 1836-'37.

In April, 1837, he was appointed, by President Van Buren, Register of the Land Office at Springfield. He afterward practised his profession.

In January, 1841, he was appointed Secretary of State; and in February elected a Judge of the Supreme Court. He continued as Judge, performing his duties with great and acknowledged ability until June, 1843, when he was nominated for Congress.

In December, 1843, he took his seat in Congress, being several months less than thirty years of age. In 1844 he was re-elected by 1,700 majority, and in 1846 by over 3,000 majority; but after the last election, and before the commencement of his term under it, he was elected a Senator of the United States.

Mr. Douglas was an active and ardent supporter of the American title up to the line of 54° 40' on the Oregon boundary question, and was one of the last to surrender.

He was also a supporter of the annexation of Texas. Mr. Douglas voted steadily, up to 1850, against the reception of abolition petitions. He was a firm advocate of the extension of the 36° 30' line to the Pacific Ocean. He voted, during the same period, against the Wilmot proviso.

In 1849–'50 the Legislature of Illinois instructed him to vote for the prohibition of slavery in the Territories; he voted in accordance with these instructions—protesting, however, that the votes were not his, but were the votes of those who had instructed him.

He supported the Fugitive Slave Act. In 1854 he proposed the Kansas-Nebraska Act, repealing the Missouri restriction upon slavery north of 36° 30', on the ground that Congress, in 1850, had declared that thenceforth the question of slavery in the Territories should be left exclusively to the determination of the people settled therein. He carried this measure through Congress in the face of all opposition.

In 1856 Mr. Douglas took the stump in behalf of Mr. Buchanan and the Cincinnati platform, and succeeded in securing the vote of Illinois for the Cincinnati nominees.

In 1857 the Lecompton controversy arose. Mr. Douglas thought that, under a strict adherence to Democratic faith, Congress ought not to accept a constitution unless it was the act of the people. The President thought differently. The Lecompton controversy arose. In the final settlement of the controversy Mr. Douglas acquiesced, but his enemies sought his destruction. They opposed his re-election in 1858; but, after one of the most eventful political contests in the Union, Mr. Douglas carried the State Legislature, and in January, 1859, was re-elected to the Senate.

HERSCHEL V. JOHNSON,

OF GEORGIA.

—————•—————

HERSCHEL V. JOHNSON was born in Burke county, Ga., on the 18th of September, 1812. In early life he enjoyed all the facilities for intellectual improvement which his native county afforded. At public schools he was prepared for college, and in January, 1831, became a member of the Freshman class in the University of Georgia, and graduated in 1834. Selecting the law as his profession, many of his leisure hours, while in college, were devoted to its study, and for months before his graduation, he repaired to the law school of Judge Gould, in Augusta, where, while attending a course of law lectures, he reviewed the college studies in which his class was engaged. By this double tax upon his physical and intellectual energies, he was enabled to stand his examination in college in August, and in September following was admitted to the bar.

He opened an office in Augusta, where he pursued his profession until 1839, when he removed to Jefferson county, and soon acquired an extensive and lucrative practice. Like most young men of our country, political life held out to him its allurements, and with little resistance on his part he soon found himself engulfed in its vortex. Educated in the principles of Democracy, he entertained sentiments of profound respect for them, and for all who consistently maintained them. Through the press and on the stump, in the ever memorable race between Van Buren and Harrison, he did his party important services. The gallant Glascock, who was then in the meridian of his renown, and who often witnessed his exploits, spoke of him as a youthful giant, who fought with burnished armor, and was able to compete with the most stalwart of his foes. In June, 1841, in a State Convention of the Democratic party, held in Milledgeville, for

2

the purpose of nominating candidates for Congress (the State then electing by general ticket), Mr. Johnson was brought forward as a candidate for a seat. He, however, being a member of the Convention, withdrew his name in favor of Howell Cobb.

In the spring of 1844, he located in the vicinity of Milledgeville. The State, at this time, was divided into congressional districts, and Mr. Polk having been nominated for the Presidency, Mr. Johnson was unanimously selected by the Democratic Convention as the elector for the Seventh district.

He was appointed to the United States Senate, and took his seat in that body on the 14th of February, 1848, and sustained the measures of Mr. Polk's administration.

He was a delegate to the National Democratic Convention, held at Baltimore in June, 1848. On his return to Georgia, after the adjournment of Congress, he participated in the Presidential canvass then in progress. On reassuming his seat in the Senate, in December, he was elected chairman of the Committee on the District of Columbia. The career of Colonel Johnson in the United States Senate was brief, but it was brilliant. It was no small compliment to him that he stood high in the estimation of John C. Calhoun—that distinguished senator having more than once declared he regarded him the ablest man of his age then in the Senate.

In November, 1859, he was elected by the Legislature of Georgia, Judge of the Superior Court for the Ocmulgee District. In this new and responsible position, he did not disappoint the expectations of those who placed him in it.

Having been nominated a candidate for Governor, he resigned his seat on the bench in August, 1853, was elected Governor on the first Monday of October, and inaugurated on the 9th of November.

Judge Johnson, besides his political speeches, has, on several occasions, distinguished himself by his efforts in other fields.

As a public speaker, he enjoys an enviable reputation. On the hustings he has few equals. As a man, Judge Johnson's public and private character is without a stain.

Without any adventitious circumstances to aid him, by mere force of talent and weight of character, he has won his way to a proud distinction among the leading spirits of the country.

NATIONAL DEMOCRATIC (Douglas) PLATFORM,

PUT FORTH AT CHARLESTON, APRIL, 1860, AND AT BALTIMORE, JUNE
23, 1860.

Resolved, That we, the Democracy of the Union, in Convention assembled, do hereby declare our affirmation of the resolutions unanimously adopted and declared as a platform of principles by the Democratic Convention at Cincinnati, in the year 1856, believing that Democratic principles are unchangeable in their nature when applied to the same subject matters.

Resolved, That it is the duty of the United States to afford ample and complete protection to all citizens, whether at home or abroad, and whether native or foreign born.

Resolved, That one of the necessities of the age, in a military, commercial, and postal point of view, is speedy communication between the Atlantic and Pacific States, and the Democratic party pledge such constitutional power of the Government as will insure the construction of a railroad to the Pacific coast at the earliest practicable period.

Resolved, That the Democratic party are in favor of the acquisition of Cuba on such terms as shall be honorable to ourselves and just to Spain.

Resolved, That the enactments of State Legislatures to defeat the faithful execution of the Fugitive Slave Law, are hostile in character and subversive to the Constitution, and revolutionary in their effects.

Resolved, That it is in accordance with the Cincinnati Platform, that during the existence of Territorial Governments the measure of restriction, whatever it may be, imposed by the Federal Constitution on the power of the Territorial Legislature over the subject of the domestic relations, as the same has been, or shall hereafter be finally determined by the Supreme Court of the United States, should be respected by all good citizens, and enforced with promptness and fidelity by every branch of the General Government.

John C. Breckinridge

JOHN C. BRECKINRIDGE,

———————

JOHN C. BRECKINRIDGE was born near Lexington, Kentucky, January 16, 1821. His father was an eminent clergyman ; his grandfather served a term as United States Senator, and filled the office of Attorney-General of the United States.

Mr. Breckinridge received his education at Centre College, enjoyed the benefits of some months at Princeton, studied law at Transylvania Institute, and was admitted to the bar at Lexington. He emigrated to the Northwest, but, after something less that two years spent in Burlington, Iowa, he returned to his native State, and took up his abode at Lexington, where he still resides. He entered immediately on the practice of his profession, and met with a well-merited success.

The trump of war, however, excited his military ardor, and the result was creditable service as a major of infantry during the Mexican War. He also distinguished himself as the counsel for Major-General Pillow in the celebrated court-martial of that officer.

On the return of Major Breckinridge from Mexico, he was elected to the Kentucky Legislature, and created so favorable an impression as a legislator that he was elected to Congress from the Ashland District, and, being re-elected, held his seat from 1851 to 1855.

His career in Congress was marked by a devoted attention to his duties as a legislator.

In the Thirty-second Congress he was instrumental in securing an appropriation for the completion of a cemetery near the city of Mexico, in which the remains of the American officers and soldiers who fell in battle, or otherwise, in or near the city of Mexico, should be interred. He also favored an appropriation for a weekly mail with the Pacific, and advocated putting these contracts to the lowest bidder.

During the angry sessions of the Thirty-third Congress Mr. Breckinridge took an active part, as one of the Administration leaders, and was drawn into a quarrel with Mr. Cutting, of New-York, which very nearly ended in a duel. Shortly after this affair—in which Mr. Breckinridge's coolness and firmness were highly commended—President Pierce tendered to him the mission to Spain ; but the honor was respectfully declined, family matters compelling Mr. Breckinridge to this course. He was a delegate to the Cincinnati Convention in June, 1856. Mr. Breckinridge was nominated for Vice-President on the ticket with Mr. Buchanan, and was elected to that office in November, 1856. Thus, at the age of thirty-five, he had served his country abroad, had been a legislator in his State and in the National Legislature, had been tendered the representation of the Republic in Europe, and elevated to the second office in the gift of the people.

As President of the United States Senate, he took the chair of that eminent body early in the first session of the Thirty-fifth Congress, December, 1857, and, with some intermission, caused by the illness of his family, presided during that stormy session.

At the last session of the Kentucky Legislature, Mr. Breckinridge received the unsought-for nomination of his party for the United States Senate. He was elected to succeed Hon. John J. Crittenden, from the fourth of March, 1861, by twenty-nine majority on joint ballot. His senatorial term would expire in 1867, had not the people determined to elevate him to a higher position.

Mr. Breckinridge possesses all those personal traits which endear the man as much to the masses as to his more immediate friends. He is a courtly and polished gentleman, chivalrous and high-toned, the very soul of honor, a second Bayard in the battle-field, a man of intellect, honest and straightforward in the expression of his opinions, no politician, no wire-puller, no trickster, prompt in decision, quick in execution, a very lion of the tribe of Jackson. He is by far the youngest of the more prominent men in the country, and it is with no little pride that his State, and his friends throughout the United States, may point to that fact.

JOSEPH LANE,

OF OREGON.

———◆———

JOSEPH LANE, the second son of John Lane and Elizabeth Street, was born in North Carolina, on the 14th of December, 1801. In 1804, the father emigrated to Kentucky and settled in Henderson county. At an early age he shifted for himself, and entered the employ of Nathaniel Hart, Clerk of the County Court. In 1816, he went into Warwick county, Indiana, became a clerk in a mercantile house, married, in 1820, a young girl of French and Irish extraction, and settled on the banks of the Ohio, in Vanderburg county.

Young Lane soon became the man of the people among whom he had cast his lot. In 1822, then barely eligible, he was elected to the Indiana Legislature, and took his seat, to the astonishment of many older worthies.

As farmer, produce-dealer, and legislator, many years rolled over his head, every year adding to his popularity as a man, both in his private and public capacity. He was frequently re-elected by the people, and continued to serve them, at short intervals, in either branch of the Legislature, for a period of twenty-four years.

In politics, General Lane has always been of the Jefferson and Jackson school. Possessing a strong intellect, and a memory retentive of facts, and quick to use them, he has become thoroughly acquainted with the history and politics of the country. He supported Jackson in 1824, '28, and '32 ; gave his voice and energies for Van Buren in 1836 and '40, and Polk in 1844.

In the spring of 1846, the war commenced between the United States and Mexico. Lane, then a member of the State Senate, immediately resigned, and entered Captain Walker's company as a private.

At Saltillo, he was made civil and military commandant of that post by Major General Butler.

The famous battle of Buena Vista was fought on the 22d and 23d of February, 1847. General Lane was third in command. From the beginning to the end he was in the hottest of the fight.

The battle of Tehualtaplan was the last fought in Mexico. Peace was soon declared, but General Lane remained some months directing the movements consequent upon the return of our troops.

About the 1st of August, 1848, General Lane reached Indiana. On the 18th, he was appointed Governor of Oregon. On the 28th his commission reached him, and on the next day he set out for his post.

On the 2d of March, 1849, about six months after his departure from home, he arrived safely in Oregon City.

As Delegate from Oregon, General Lane was unremitting in his advocacy of the interests of the Territory, and untiring in his efforts for her admission into the Union.

While Governor Lane was in Oregon, he was named for the Presidency by the Convention assembled at Indianapolis to revise the State Constitution of Indiana. The Democratic State Convention, which met February 24, 1852, formally presented his claims for the Chief-Magistracy, pledging the vote of the State to him.

Gen. Lane has been the artificer of his own fortunes ; and, in his progress from the farmer on the banks of the Ohio, and the commandant of a flat-boat, to posts of honorable distinction—to a seat in the House of Representatives and in the Senate of Indiana—to the command of a brigade upon the fields of Buena Vista, Huamantla and at Atlixco—to the Governorship of Oregon, and thence to a seat in Congress— in all he has displayed the same high characteristics, perseverance, and energy.

NATIONAL DEMOCRATIC (Breckinridge) PLATFORM,

PUT FORTH AT CHARLESTON, APRIL 30, 1860, AND AT BALTIMORE, JUNE 23, 1860.

Resolved, That the platform adopted by the Democratic party at Cincinnati is affirmed, with the following explanatory resolutions:

First—That the government of a Territory organized by an act of Congress is provisional and temporary, and during its existence all citizens of the United States have an equal right to settle with their property in the Territory, without their rights, either of person or property, being destroyed or injured by Congressional or Territorial legislation.

Second—That it is the duty of the Federal Government, in all its departments, to protect, when necessary, the rights of persons and property in the Territories, and wherever else its constitutional authority extends.

Third—That when the settlers in a Territory, having an adequate population, form a State Constitution, the right of sovereignty commences, and being consummated by admission into the Union, they stand on an equal footing with the people of other States; and a State thus organized ought to be admitted into the Federal Union, whether its Constitution prohibits or recognizes the institution of slavery.

Resolved, That the Democratic party are in favor of the acquisition of the island of Cuba, on such terms as shall be honorable to ourselves and just to Spain, at the earliest practicable moment.

Resolved, That the enactments of State Legislatures to defeat the faithful execution of the Fugitive Slave Law, are hostile in character to, and subversive of, the Constitution, and revolutionary in their effect.

Resolved, That the Democracy of the United States recognize it as an imperative duty of the Government to protect naturalized citizens in all their rights, whether at home or in foreign lands, to the same extent as its native-born citizens. And,

Whereas, One of the greatest necessities of the age, in a political, commercial, postal, and military point of view, is a speedy communication between the Pacific and Atlantic coasts; therefore, be it

Resolved, That the National Democratic party do hereby pledge themselves to use every means in their power to secure the passage of some bill, to the extent of the constitutional authority of Congress, for the construction of a Pacific Railroad from the Mississippii River or the Pacific Ocean, at the earliest practicable moment.

THE CINCINNATI PLATFORM,

PUT FORTH MAY 22, 1856.

Resolved, That the American Democracy place their trust in the intelligence, the patriotism, and the discriminating justice of the American people.

Resolved, That we regard this as a distinctive feature of our political creed, which we are proud to maintain before the world as a great moral element in a form of government springing from and upheld by the popular will; and we contrast it with the creed and practice of Federalism, under whatever name or form, which seeks to palsy the will of the constituent, and which conceives no imposture too monstrous for the popular credulity.

Resolved, Therefore, that entertaining these views, the Democratic party of this Union, through their delegates, assembled in general Convention, coming together in a spirit of concord, of devotion to the doctrines and faith of a free representative government, and appealing to their fellow-citizens for the rectitude of their intentions, renew and reassert before the American people, the declarations of principles avowed by them, when, on former occasions, in general Convention, they have presented their candidates for the popular suffrage.

1. That the Federal Government is one of limited power, derived solely from the Constitution, and the grants of power made therein ought to be strictly construed by all the departments and agents of the Government; that it is inexpedient and dangerous to exercise doubtful constitutional powers.

2. That the Constitution does not confer upon the General Government the power to commence and carry on a general system of internal improvements.

3. That the Constitution does not confer authority upon the Federal Government, directly or indirectly, to assume the debts of the several States, contracted for local and internal improvements, or other State purposes, nor would such assumption be just or expedient.

4. That justice and sound policy forbid the Federal Government to foster one branch of industry to the detriment of another, or to cherish the interest of one portion of our common country; that

every citizen and every section of the country has a right to demand and insist upon au equality of rights and privileges, and a complete and ample protection of persons and property from domestic violence and foreign aggression.

5. That it is the duty of every branch of the Government to enforce and practise the most rigid economy in conducting our public affairs, and that no more revenue ought to be raised than is required to defray the necessary expenses of the Government and gradual but certain extinction of the public debt.

6. That the proceeds of the public lands ought to be sacredly applied to the national objects specified in the Constitution, and that we are opposed to any law for the distribution of such proceeds among the States, as alike inexpedient in policy and repugnant to the Constitution.

7. That Congress has no power to charter a National Bank ; that we believe such an institution one of deadly hostility to the best interests of this country, dangerous to our Republican institutions and the liberties of the people, and calculated to place the business of the country within the control of a consecrated money power and above the laws and will of the people ; and the results of the Democratic legislation in this and in all other financial measures, upon which issues have been made between the two political parties of the country, have demonstrated to candid and practical men of all parties their soundness, safety, and utility in all business pursuits.

8. That the separation of the moneys of the Government from banking institutions, is indispensable to the safety of the funds of the Government and the rights of the people.

9. That we are decidedly opposed to taking from the President the qualified Veto power, by which he is enabled. under restrictions and responsibilities amply sufficient to guard the public interests, to suspend the passage of a bill whose merits cannot secure the approval of two thirds of the Senate and House of Representatives, until the judgment of the people can be obtained thereon ; and which has saved the American people from the corrupt and tyrannical dominion of the bank of the United States, and from a corrupting system of general internal improvements.

10. That the liberal principles embodied by Jefferson in the Declaration of Independence, and sanctioned by the Constitution, which makes ours the land of liberty and the asylum of the oppressed of every nation, have ever been cardinal principles in the Democratic faith ; and every attempt to abridge the privilege of becoming citizens and the owners of soil among us ought to be resisted with the same spirit which swept the alien and sedition laws from our statute-books.

And whereas, Since the foregoing declaration was uniformly adopted by our predecessors in National Convention, an adverse political and religious test has been secretly organized by a party claiming to be exclusively Americans, and it is proper that the American Democracy should define its relations thereto ; and declares its determined opposition to all secret political societies, by whatever name they may be called,

Resolved, That the foundation of this Union of States having been laid in, and its prosperity, expansion, and pre-eminent example in free government, built upon entire freedom of matters of religious concernment, and no respect of persons in regard to rank, or place of birth, no party can justly be deemed national, constitutional, or in accordance with American principles, which bases its exclusive organization upon religious opinions and accidental birthplace. And hence a political crusade in the nineteenth century, and in the United States of America, against Catholics and foreign-born, is neither justified by the past history or future prospects of the country, nor in unison with the spirit of toleration and enlightened freedom which peculiarly distinguishes the American system of popular government.

Resolved, That we reiterate with renewed energy of purpose the well-considered declarations of former conventions upon the sectional issue of domestic Slavery, and concerning the reserved rights of the States—

1. That Congress has no power under the Constitution to interfere with or control the domestic institutions of the several States, and that all such States are the sole and proper judges of everything appertaining to their own affairs not prohibited by the Constitution ; that all efforts of the Abolitionists or others made to induce Congress to interfere with questions of slavery, or to take incipient steps in relation thereto, are calculated to lead to the most alarming and dangerous consequences ; and that all such efforts have an inevitable tendency to diminish the happiness of the people, and endanger the stability and permanency of the Union, and ought not to be countenanced by any friend of our political institutions.

2. That the foregoing proposition covers and was intended to embrace the whole subject of slavery agitation in Congress, and, therefore, the Democratic party of the Union, standing on this national platform, will abide by and adhere to a faithful execution of the acts known as the Compromise measures, settled by the Congress of 1850 : " The act for reclaiming fugitives from service or labor included ;" which act being designed to carry out an express provision of the Constitution, cannot, with fidelity thereto, be repealed or so changed as to destroy or impair its efficiency.

3. That the Democratic party will resist all attempts at renewing in Congress, or out of it, the agitation of the Slavery question, under whatever shape or color the attempt may be made.

4. That the Democratic party will faithfully abide by and uphold the principles laid down in the Kentucky and Virginia resolutions of 1792 and 1798, and in the report of Mr. Madison to the Virginia legislature in 1799—that it adopts these principles as constituting one of the main foundations of its political creed, and is resolved to carry them out in their obvious meaning and import.

And that we may more distinctly meet the issue on which a sectional party, subsisting exclusively on Slavery agitation, now relies to test the fidelity of the people, North and South, to the Constitution and the Union :

1. *Resolved*, That claiming fellowship with and desiring the co-operation of all who regard the preservation of the Union under the Constitution, as the paramount issue, and repudiating all sectional parties and platforms concerning domestic slavery, which seek to embroil the States, and incite to treason and armed resistance to law in the territories, and whose avowed purpose, if consummated. must end in civil war and disunion, the American Democracy recognize and adopt the principles contained in the organic laws establishing the Territories of Nebraska and Kansas, as embodying the only sound and safe solution of the Slavery question, upon which the great national idea of the people of this whole country can repose in its determined conservation of the Union, and non-interference of Congress with Slavery in the Territories or in the District of Columbia.

2. That this was the basis of the compromises of 1850, confirmed by both the Democratic and Whig parties in National Conventions, ratified by the people in the election of 1852, and rightly applied to the organization of the Territories in 1854.

3. That by the uniform application of the Democratic principle to the organization of Territories, and the admission of new States, with or without domestic Slavery, as they may elect, the equal rights of all the States will be preserved intact, the original compacts of the Constitution maintained inviolate, and the perpetuity and expansion of the Union insured to its utmost capacity of embracing, in peace and harmony, every future American State that may be constituted or annexed with a Republican form of government.

Resolved, That we recognize the right of the people of all the Territories, including Kansas and Nebraska, acting through the legally and fairly expressed will of the majority of the actual residents, and whenever the number of their inhabitants justifies it, to form a Constitution, with or without Domestic Slavery, and be admitted into the Union upon terms of perfect equality with the other States.

Resolved, finally, That, in view of the condition of the popular institutions in the Old World (and the dangerous tendencies of sectional agitation, combined with the attempt to enforce civil and religious disabilities against the rights of acquiring and enjoying citizenship in our own land), a high and sacred duty is involved, with increased responsibility, upon the Democratic party of this country, as the party of the Union, to uphold and maintain the rights of every State, and thereby the Union of the States—and to sustain and advance among us constitutional liberty, by continuing to resist all monopolies and exclusive legislation for the benefit of the few at the expense of the many, and by a vigilant and constant adherence to those principles and compromises of the Constitution—which are broad enough and strong enough to embrace and uphold the Union as it was, the Union as it is, and the Union as it shall be—in the full expression of the energies and capacity of this great and progressive people.

1. *Resolved*, That there are questions connected with the foreign policy of this country which are inferior to no domestic question whatever. The time has come for the people of the United States to declare themselves in favor of free seas, and progressive free trade throughout the world, and, by solemn manifestations, to place their moral influence at the side of their successful example.

2. *Resolved*, That our geographical and political position, with reference to the other States of this continent, no less than the interest of our commerce and the development of our growing power, requires that we should hold sacred the principles involved in the Monroe doctrine. Their bearing and import admit of no misconstruction, and should be applied with unbending rigidity.

3. *Resolved*, That the great highway, which Nature as well as the assent of States most immediately interested in its maintenance has marked out for free communication between the Atlantic and the Pacific oceans, constitutes one of the most important achievements realized by the spirit of modern times, in the unconquerable energy of our people; and that result would be secured by a timely and efficient exertion of the control which we have the right to claim over it, and no power on earth should be suffered to impede or clog its progress by any interference with relations that it may suit our policy to establish between our government and the governments of the States within whose dominions it lies; we can, under no circumstances, surrender our preponderance in the adjustment of all questions arising out of it.

4. *Resolved*, That in view of so commanding an interest, the people of the United States cannot but sympathize with the efforts which are being made by the people of Central America to regenerate that portion of the continent which covers the passage across the interoceanic isthmus.

5. *Resolved*, That the Democratic party will expect of the next administration that every proper effort be made to insure our ascendency in the Gulf of Mexico, and to maintain permanent protection to the great outlets through which are emptied into its waters the products raised out of the soil and the commodities created by the industry of the people of our Western valleys and of the Union at large.

CONSTITUTION

OF THE

UNITED STATES OF AMERICA.

WE the People of the United States, in order to form a more perfect Union, establish Justice, insure domestic Tranquillity, provide for the common Defence, promote the general Welfare, and secure the Blessings of Liberty to ourselves and our Posterity, do ordain and establish this CONSTITUTION for the United States of America.

ARTICLE I.

SECTION I.

All legislative Powers herein granted shall be vested in a Congress of the United States, which shall consist of a Senate and House of Representatives.

SECTION II.

1. The House of Representatives shall be composed of Members chosen every second Year by the People of the several States, and the Electors in each State shall have the Qualifications requisite for Electors of the most numerous Branch of the State Legislature.

2. No Person shall be a Representative who shall not have attained to the Age of twenty-five Years, and been seven Years a Citizen of the United States, and who shall not, when elected, be an Inhabitant of that State in which he shall be chosen.

3. Representatives and direct Taxes shall be apportioned among the several States which may be included within this Union, according to their respective Numbers, which shall be determined by adding to the whole Number of free Persons, including those bound to Service for a Term of Years, and excluding Indians not taxed, three fifths of all other Persons. The actual Enumeration shall be made within three Years after the first Meeting of the Congress of the United States, and within every subsequent Term of ten Years, in such manner as they shall by Law direct. The Number of Representatives shall not exceed one for every thirty Thousand, but each State shall have at least one Representative; and until such enumeration shall be made, the State of New Hampshire shall be entitled to chuse three, Massachusetts eight, Rhode

Island and Providence Plantations one, Connecticut five, New York six, New Jersey four, Pennsylvania eight, Delaware one, Maryland, six, Virginia ten, North Carolina five, South Carolina five, and Georgia three.

4. When Vacancies happen in the Representation from any State, the Executive Authority thereof shall issue writs of Election to fill such Vacancies.

5. The House of Representatives shall chuse their Speaker and other Officers; and shall have the sole Power of Impeachment.

SECTION III.

1. The Senate of the United States shall be composed of two Senators from each State, chosen by the Legislature thereof, for six Years; and each Senator shall have one Vote.

2. Immediately after they shall be assembled in Consequence of the first Election, they shall be divided as equally as may be into three Classes. The Seats of the Senators of the first Class shall be vacated at the Expiration of the second Year, of the second Class at the Expiration of the fourth Year, and of the third Class at the Expiration of the sixth year, so that one-third may be chosen every second Year; and if Vacancies happen by Resignation, or otherwise, during the Recess of the Legislature of any State, the Executive thereof may make temporary Appointments until the next Meeting of the Legislature, which shall then fill such Vacancies.

3. No Person shall be a Senator who shall not have attained to the Age of thirty Years, and been nine Years a Citizen of the United States, and who shall not, when elected, be an Inhabitant of that State for which he shall be chosen.

4. The Vice President of the United States shall be President of the Senate, but shall have no Vote, unless they be equally divided.

5. The Senate shall chuse their other Officers, and also a President pro tempore, in the Absence of the Vice President, or when he shall exercise the Office of President of the United States.

6. The Senate shall have the sole Power to try all Impeachments. When sitting for that Purpose, they shall be on Oath or Affirmation. When the President of the United States is tried, the Chief Justice shall preside: And no Person shall be convicted without the Concurrence of two thirds of the Members present.

7. Judgment in Cases of Impeachment shall not extend further than to removal from Office, and Disqualification to hold and enjoy any Office of Honour, Trust or Profit under the United States: but the Party convicted shall nevertheless be liable and subject to Indictment, Trial, Judgment and Punishment according to Law.

SECTION IV.

1. The Times, Places and Manner of holding Elections for Senators and Representatives, shall be prescribed in each State by the Legislature thereof; but the Congress may at any time by Law

make or alter such regulations, except as to the places of chusing Senators.

2. The Congress shall assemble at least once in every Year, and such Meeting shall be on the first Monday in December, unless they shall by Law appoint a different Day.

SECTION V.

1. Each House shall be the Judge of the Elections, Returns and Qualifications of its own Members, and a Majority of each shall constitute a Quorum to do Business; but a smaller Number may adjourn from day to day, and may be authorized to compel the Attendance of absent Members, in such Manner, and under such Penalties as each House may provide.

2. Each House may determine the Rules of its Proceedings, punish its Members for disorderly Behaviour, and, with the Concurrence of two thirds, expel a Member.

3. Each House shall keep a Journal of its Proceedings, and from time to time publish the same, excepting such Parts as may in their Judgment require Secrecy; and the Yeas and Nays of the Members of either House on any question shall, at the Desire of one fifth of those Present, be entered on the Journal.

4. Neither House, during the Session of Congress, shall, without the Consent of the other, adjourn for more than three Days, nor to any other place than that in which the two Houses shall be sitting.

SECTION VI.

1. The Senators and Representatives shall receive a Compensation for their Services, to be ascertained by Law, and paid out of the Treasury of the United States. They shall in all Cases, except Treason, Felony, and Breach of the Peace, be privileged from Arrest during their Attendance at the Session of their respective Houses, and in going to and returning from the same; and for any Speech or Debate in either House, they shall not be questioned in any other Place.

2. No Senator or Representative shall, during the Time for which he was elected, be appointed to any civil Office under the Authority of the United States, which shall have been created, or the Emoluments whereof shall have been increased during such time; and no Person holding any Office under the United States, shall be a Member of either House during his Continuance in Office.

SECTION VII.

1. All Bills for raising Revenue shall originate in the House of Representatives; but the Senate may propose or concur with Amendments as on other Bills.

2. Every Bill which shall have passed the House of Representatives and the Senate, shall, before it become a Law, be presented to the President of the United States; If he approve he shall sign it, but if not, he shall return it, with his Objections to that House

in which it shall have originated, who shall enter the Objections at large on their Journal, and proceed to reconsider it. If after such Reconsideration two thirds of that House shall agree to pass the Bill, it shall be sent, together with the Objections, to the other House, by which it shall likewise be reconsidered, and if approved by two thirds of that House, it shall become a Law. But in all such Cases the Votes of both Houses shall be determined by Yeas and Nays, and the Names of the Persons voting for and against the Bill shall be entered on the Journal of each House respectively. If any Bill shall not be returned by the President within ten Days (Sundays excepted) after it shall have been presented to him, the Same shall be a law, in like Manner as if he had signed it, unless the Congress by their Adjournment prevent its Return, in which Case it shall not be a Law.

3. Every Order, Resolution, or Vote to which the Concurrence of the Senate and House of Representatives may be necessary (except on a question of Adjournment) shall be presented to the President of the United States; and before the Same shall take Effect, shall be approved by him, or being disapproved by him, shall be repassed by two thirds of the Senate and House of Representatives, according to the Rules and Limitations prescribed in the Case of a Bill.

SECTION VIII.

The Congress shall have Power

1. To lay and collect Taxes, Duties, Imposts and Excises, to pay the Debts and provide for the common Defence and general Welfare of the United States; but all Duties, Imposts and Excises shall be uniform throughout the United States;

2. To borrow Money on the credit of the United States;

3. To regulate Commerce with foreign Nations, and among the several States, and with the Indian Tribes;

4. To establish an uniform Rule of Naturalization, and uniform Laws on the subject of Bankruptcies throughout the United States;

5. To coin Money, regulate the Value thereof, and of foreign Coin, and fix the Standard of Weights and Measures;

6. To provide for the Punishment of counterfeiting the Securities and current coin of the United States;

7. To establish Post Offices and Post Roads;

8. To promote the progress of Science and useful Arts, by securing for limited Times to Authors and Inventors the exclusive Right to their respective Writings and Discoveries;

9. To constitute Tribunals inferior to the supreme Court;

10. To define and punish Piracies and Felonies committed on the high Seas, and Offences against the Law of Nations;

11. To declare War, grant Letters of Marque and Reprisal, and make Rules concerning Captures on Land and Water;

12. To raise and support Armies, but no Appropriation of Money to that Use shall be for a longer Term than two Years;

13. To provide and maintain a Navy;

14. To make Rules for the Government and Regulation of the land and naval Forces;

15. To provide for calling forth the Militia to execute the Laws of the Union, suppress Insurrections and repel Invasions;

16. To provide for organizing, arming, and disciplining, the Militia, and for governing such Part of them as may be employed in the Service of the United States, reserving to the States respectively, the Appointment of the Officers, and the Authority of training the Militia according to the Discipline prescribed by Congress;

17. To exercise exclusive Legislation in all Cases whatsoever, over such District (not exceeding ten Miles square) as may, by Cession of particular States, and the Acceptance of Congress, become the Seat of the Government of the United States, and to exercise like Authority over all Places purchased by the Consent of the Legislature of the State in which the Same shall be, for the Erection of Forts, Magazines, Arsenals, Dock-Yards, and other needful Buildings;—And

18. To make all Laws which shall be necessary and proper for carrying into Execution the foregoing Powers, and all other Powers vested by this Constitution in the Government of the United States, or in any Department or Officer thereof.

SECTION IX.

1. The Migration or Importation of such Persons as any of the States now existing shall think proper to admit, shall not be prohibited by the Congress prior to the Year one thousand eight hundred and eight, but a Tax or Duty may be imposed on such Importation, not exceeding ten dollars for each Person.

2. The Privilege of the Writ of Habeas Corpus shall not be suspended, unless when in Cases of Rebellion or Invasion the public Safety may require it.

3. No Bill of Attainder or ex post facto Law shall be passed.

4. No Capitation, or other direct, Tax shall be laid, unless in Proportion to the Census or Enumeration herein before directed to be taken.

5. No Tax or Duty shall be laid on Articles exported from any State.

6. No Preference shall be given by any Regulation of Commerce or Revenue to the Ports of one State over those of another: nor shall Vessels bound to, or from, one State, be obliged to enter, clear, or pay Duties in another.

7. No Money shall be drawn from the Treasury, but in Consequence of Appropriations made by Law; and a regular Statement and Account of the Receipts and Expenditures of all public Money shall be published from time to time.

8. No Title of Nobility shall be granted by the United States: And no Person holding any Office of Profit or Trust under them, shall, without the Consent of the Congress, accept of any Present,

Emolument, Office, or Title, of any kind whatever, from any King, Prince, or foreign State.

SECTION X.

1. No State shall enter into any Treaty, Alliance, or Confederation; grant Letters of Marque and Reprisal; coin Money; emit Bills of Credit; make any Thing but gold and silver Coin a Tender in payment of Debts; pass any Bill of Attainder, ex post facto Law, or Law impairing the Obligation of Contracts, or grant any Title of Nobility.

2. No State shall, without the consent of the Congress, lay any Imposts or Duties on Imports or Exports, except what may be absolutely necessary for executing its inspection Laws: and the net Produce of all Duties and Imposts, laid by any State on Imports or Exports, shall be for the Use of the Treasury of the United States; and all such Laws shall be subject to the Revision and Controul of the Congress.

3. No State shall, without the Consent of Congress, lay any Duty of Tonnage, keep Troops, or Ships of War in time of Peace, enter into any Agreement or Compact with another State, or with a foreign Power, or engage in War, unless actually invaded, or in such imminent Danger as will not admit of Delay.

ARTICLE II.

SECTION I.

1. The executive Power shall be vested in a President of the United States of America. He shall hold his Office during the Term of four Years, and, together with the Vice President, chosen for the same Term, be elected as follows:

2. Each State shall appoint, in such Manner as the Legislature thereof may direct, a Number of Electors, equal to the whole Number of Senators and Representatives to which the State may be entitled in the Congress: but no Senator or Representative, or Person holding an Office of Trust or Profit under the United States, shall be appointed an Elector.

[* The Electors shall meet in their respective States, and vote by Ballot for two Persons, of whom one at least shall not be an Inhabitant of the same State with themselves. And they shall make a List of all the Persons voted for, and of the Number of Votes for each; which List they shall sign and certify, and transmit sealed to the Seat of the Government of the United States, directed to the President of the Senate. The President of the Senate shall, in the Presence of the Senate and House of Representatives, open all the Certificates, and the Votes shall then be counted. The Person having the greatest Number of Votes shall be the President, if such Number be a Majority of the whole Number of Electors appointed; and if there be more than one who have such Majority, and have an equal Number of Votes, then the House of Representatives shall immediately chuse by Ballot one of them for President; and if no Person have a Majority, then from the five highest on the List, the said House shall in like manner chuse the President. But in chusing the President, the Votes shall be taken by States, the Representation

* This clause within brackets has been superseded and annulled by the 12th amendment, on page 462.

from each State having one Vote; A Quorum for this Purpose shall consist of a Member or Members from two thirds of the States, and a Majority of all the States shall be necessary to a Choice. In every Case, after the Choice of the President, the Person having the greatest Number of Votes of the Electors shall be the Vice President. But if there should remain two or more who have equal Votes, the Senate shall chuse from them by Ballot the Vice President.]

3. The Congress may determine the Time of chusing the Electors, and the Day on which they shall give their Votes; which Day shall be the same throughout the United States.

4. No Person except a natural born Citizen, or a Citizen of the United States at the time of the Adoption of this Constitution, shall be eligible to the Office of President; neither shall any Person be eligible to that Office who shall not have attained to the Age of thirty five Years, and been fourteen Years a Resident within the United States.

5. In Case of the Removal of the President from Office, or of his Death, Resignation, or Inability to discharge the Powers and Duties of the said Office, the same shall devolve on the Vice President, and the Congress may by Law provide for the Case of Removal, Death, Resignation, or Inability, both of the President and Vice President, declaring what Officer shall then act as President, and such Officer shall act accordingly, until the Disability be removed, or a President shall be elected.

6. The President shall, at stated Times, receive for his Services, a Compensation, which shall neither be increased nor diminished during the Period for which he shall have been elected, and he shall not receive within that Period, any other Emolument from the United States, or any of them.

7. Before he enter on the Execution of his Office, he shall take the following Oath or Affirmation:—

"I do solemnly swear (or affirm) that I will faithfully execute "the Office of President of the United States, and will to the best "of my Ability, preserve, protect and defend the Constitution of "the United States."

SECTION II.

1. The President shall be Commander in Chief of the Army and Navy of the United States, and of the Militia of the several States, when called into the actual Service of the United States; he may require the Opinion, in writing, of the principal Officer in each of the executive Departments, upon any subject relating to the Duties of their respective Offices, and he shall have Power to grant Reprieves and Pardons for Offences against the United States, except in Cases of Impeachment.

2. He shall have Power, by and with the Advice and Consent of the Senate, to make Treaties, provided two thirds of the Senators present concur; and he shall nominate, and by and with the Advice and Consent of the Senate, shall appoint Ambassadors, other public Ministers and Consuls, Judges of the supreme Court, and all other Officers of the United States, whose Appointments are not herein otherwise provided for, and which shall be estab-·

lished by Law: but the Congress may by Law vest the Appointment of such inferior Officers as they think proper, in the President alone, in the Courts of Law, or in the Heads of Departments.

SECTION III.

He shall from time to time give to the Congress Information of the State of the Union, and recommend to their Consideration such Measures as he shall judge necessary and expedient; he may, on extraordinary occasions, convene both Houses, or either of them, and in Case of Disagreement between them, with respect to the Time of Adjournment, he may adjourn them to such Time as he shall think proper; he shall receive Ambassadors and other public Ministers; he shall take Care that the Laws be faithfully executed, and shall Commission all the officers of the United States.

SECTION IV.

The President, Vice President, and all civil Officers of the United States, shall be removed from Office on Impeachment for, and Conviction of, Treason, Bribery, or other high Crimes and Misdemeanors.

ARTICLE III.

SECTION I.

The judicial Power of the United States shall be vested in one supreme Court, and in such inferior Courts as the Congress may from time to time ordain and establish. The Judges, both of the supreme and inferior Courts, shall hold their Offices during good Behavior, and shall, at stated Times, receive for their Services, a Compensation, which shall not be diminished during their Continuance in Office.

SECTION II.

1. The judicial Power shall extend to all Cases, in Law and Equity, arising under this Constitution, the Laws of the United States, and Treaties made, or which shall be made, under their Authority;—to all Cases affecting Ambassadors, other public Ministers, and Consuls;—to all Cases of admiralty and maritime Jurisdiction;—to Controversies to which the United States shall be a Party;—to Controversies between two or more States;—between a State and Citizens of another State;—between Citizens of different States,—between Citizens of the same State claiming Lands under Grants of different States, and between a State, or the Citizens thereof, and foreign States, Citizens or Subjects.

2. In all Cases affecting Ambassadors, other public Ministers and Consuls, and those in which a State shall be Party, the supreme Court shall have original Jurisdiction. In all the other Cases before mentioned, the supreme Court shall have appellate Jurisdiction, both as to Law and Fact, with such Exceptions, and under such Regulations as the Congress shall make

3. The Trial of all Crimes, except in Cases of Impeachment, shall be by Jury; and such Trial shall be held in the State where the said Crimes shall have been committed; but when not committed within any State, the Trial shall be at such Place or Places as the Congress may by Law have directed.

SECTION III.

1. Treason against the United States, shall consist only in levying War against them, or in adhering to their Enemies, giving them Aid and Comfort. No Person shall be convicted of Treason unless on the Testimony of two Witnesses to the same overt Act, or on Confession in open Court.

2. The Congress shall have Power to declare the Punishment of Treason, but no Attainder of Treason shall work Corruption of Blood, or Forfeiture except during the Life of the Person attainted.

ARTICLE IV.

SECTION I.

Full Faith and Credit shall be given in each State to the public Acts, Records, and judicial Proceedings of every other State. And the Congress may by general Laws prescribe the Manner in which such Acts, Records and Proceedings shall be proved, and the Effect thereof.

SECTION II.

1. The Citizens of each State shall be entitled to all Privileges and Immunities of Citizens in the several States.

2. A Person charged in any State with Treason, Felony, or other Crime, who shall flee from Justice, and be found in another State, shall on Demand of the executive Authority of the State from which he fled, be delivered up, to be removed to the State having Jurisdiction of the Crime.

3. No Person held to Service or Labour in one State, under the Laws thereof, escaping into another, shall, in Consequence of any Law or Regulation therein, be discharged from such Service or Labour, but shall be delivered up on Claim of the party to whom such Service or Labour may be due.

SECTION III.

1. New States may be admitted by the Congress into this Union; but no new State shall be formed or erected within the Jurisdiction of any other State; nor any State be formed by the Junction of two or more States, or Parts of States, without the Consent of the Legislatures of the States concerned as well as of the Congress.

2. The Congress shall have Power to dispose of and make all needful Rules and Regulations respecting the Territory or other

Property belonging to the United States; and nothing in this Constitution shall be so construed as to Prejudice any Claims of the United States, or of any particular State.

SECTION IV.

The United States shall guarantee to every State in this Union a Republican Form of Government, and shall protect each of them against Invasion; and on application of the Legislature, or of the Executive (when the Legislature cannot be convened) against domestic Violence.

ARTICLE V.

The Congress, whenever two thirds of both Houses shall deem it necessary, shall propose Amendments to this Constitution, or, on the Application of the Legislatures of two thirds of the several States, shall call a Convention for proposing Amendments, which, in either Case, shall be valid to all Intents and Purposes, as Part of this Constitution, when ratified by the Legislatures of three fourths of the several States, or by Conventions in three fourths thereof, as the one or the other Mode of Ratification may be proposed by the Congress; Provided that no Amendment which may be made prior to the Year one thousand eight hundred and eight shall in any Manner affect the first and fourth Clauses in the Ninth Section of the first Article; and that no State, without its Consent, shall be deprived of its equal Suffrage in the Senate.

ARTICLE VI.

1. All Debts contracted and Engagements entered into, before the Adoption of this Constitution, shall be as valid against the United States under this Constitution, as under the Confederation.

2. This Constitution, and the Laws of the United States which shall be made in Pursuance thereof; and all Treaties made, or which shall be made, under the authority of the United States, shall be the supreme Law of the Land; and the Judges in every State shall be bound thereby, any Thing in the Constitution or Laws of any State to the Contrary notwithstanding.

3. The Senators and Representatives before mentioned, and the Members of the several State Legislatures, and all executive and judicial Officers, both of the United States and the several States, shall be bound by Oath or Affirmation, to support this Constitution; but no religious Test shall ever be required as a Qualification to any Office or public Trust under the United States.

ARTICLE VII.

The Ratification of the Conventions of nine States, shall be sufficient for the Establishment of this Constitution between the States so ratifying the same.

DONE in Convention by the Unanimous Consent of the States present the Seventeenth Day of September in the Year of our Lord one thousand seven hundred and Eighty seven and of the Independence of the United States of America the Twelfth IN WITNESS whereof We have hereunto subscribed our Names,

GEO WASHINGTON—
Presidt and deputy from **Virginia**

NEW HAMPSHIRE.

JOHN LANGDON,   NICHOLAS GILMAN.

MASSACHUSETTS.

NATHANIEL GORHAM,   RUFUS KING.

CONNECTICUT.

WM. SAML. JOHNSON,   ROGER SHERMAN.

NEW YORK.

ALEXANDER HAMILTON.

NEW JERSEY.

WIL: LIVINGSTON,   DAVID BREARLEY,
WM. PATERSON,   JONA. DAYTON.

PENNSYLVANIA.

B. FRANKLIN,   THOMAS MIFFLIN,
ROBT. MORRIS,   GEO: CLYMER,
THO: FITSIMONS,   JARED INGERSOLL,
JAMES WILSON,   GOUV: MORRIS.

DELAWARE.

GEO: READ,   GUNNING BEDFORD, Jun'r,
JOHN DICKINSON,   RICHARD BASSETT,
JACO: BROOM.

MARYLAND.

JAMES M'HENRY,   DAN: OF ST. THOS. JENIFER,
DANL. CARROLL.

VIRGINIA.

JOHN BLAIR,   JAMES MADISON, Jr.

NORTH CAROLINA.

WM. BLOUNT,   RICH'D DOBBS SPAIGHT,
HU. WILLIAMSON.

SOUTH CAROLINA.

J. RUTLEDGE,   CHARLES COTESWORTH PINKNEY,
CHARLES PINKNEY,   PIERCE BUTLER.

GEORGIA.

WILLIAM FEW,   ABR. BALDWIN.

Attest: WILLIAM JACKSON, *Secretary.*

ARTICLES

In Addition to, and Amendment of,

THE CONSTITUTION

OF THE

UNITED STATES OF AMERICA,

Proposed by Congress, and ratified by the Legislatures of the several States, pursuant to the fifth article of the original Constitution.

ARTICLE I.

Congress shall make no law respecting an establishment of religion, or prohibiting the free exercise thereof; or abridging the freedom of speech, or of the press; or the right of the people peaceably to assemble, and to petition the Government for a redress of grievances.

ARTICLE II.

A well regulated Militia, being necessary to the security of a free State, the right of the people to keep and bear Arms, shall not be infringed.

ARTICLE III.

No Soldier shall, in time of peace, be quartered in any house, without the consent of the Owner, nor in time of war, but in a manner to be prescribed by law.

ARTICLE IV.

The right of the people to be secure in their persons, houses, papers, and effects, against unreasonable searches and seizures, shall not be violated, and no Warrants shall be issued, but upon probable cause, supported by Oath or affirmation, and particularly describing the place to be searched, and the persons or things to be seized.

ARTICLE V.

No person shall be held to answer for a capital, or otherwise infamous crime, unless on a presentment or indictment of a Grand Jury, except in cases arising in the land or naval forces, or in the Militia, when in actual service in time of War or public danger; nor shall any person be subject for the same offence to be twice put in jeopardy of life or limb; nor shall be compelled in any Criminal Case to be a witness against himself, nor be deprived of life, liberty, or property, without due process of law; nor shall private property be taken for public use, without just compensation.

ARTICLE VI.

In all criminal prosecutions, the accused shall enjoy the right to a speedy and public trial, by an impartial jury of the State and district, wherein the crime shall have been committed, which district shall have been previously ascertained by law, and to be informed of the nature and cause of the accusation; to be confronted with the witnesses against him; to have Compulsory process for obtaining Witnesses in his favor, and to have the Assistance of Counsel for his defence.

ARTICLE VII.

In Suits at common law, where the value in controversy shall exceed twenty dollars, the right of trial by jury shall be preserved, and no fact tried by a jury, shall be otherwise re-examined in any Court of the United States, than according to the rules of the common law.

ARTICLE VIII.

Excessive bail shall not be required, nor excessive fines imposed, nor cruel and unusual punishments inflicted.

ARTICLE IX.

The enumeration in the Constitution, of certain rights, shall not be construed to deny or disparage others retained by the people.

ARTICLE X.

The powers not delegated to the United States by the Constitution, nor prohibited by it to the States, are reserved to the States respectively, or to the people.

ARTICLE XI.

The Judicial power of the United States shall not be construed to extend to any suit in law or equity, commenced or prosecuted against one of the United States by Citizens of another State, or by Citizens or Subjects of any foreign State.

ARTICLE XII.

1. The Electors shall meet in their respective states, and vote by ballot for President and Vice President, one of whom, at least, shall not be an inhabitant of the same state with themselves; they shall name in their ballots the person voted for as President, and in distinct ballots the person voted for as Vice President, and they shall make distinct lists of all persons voted for as President, and of all persons voted for as Vice President, and of the number of votes for each, which lists they shall sign and certify, and transmit sealed to the seat of the government of the United States, directed to the President of the Senate;—The President of the Senate shall, in presence of the Senate and House of Representatives, open all the certificates, and the votes shall then be counted;—The person having the greatest number of votes for President, shall be the President, if such number be a majority of the whole number of Electors appointed; and if no person have such majority, then from the persons having the highest numbers not exceeding three on the list of those voted for as President, the House of Representatives shall choose immediately, by ballot, the President. But in choosing the President, the votes shall be taken by states, the representation from each state having one vote; a quorum for this purpose shall consist of a member or members from two-thirds of the states, and a majority of all the states shall be necessary to a choice. And if the House of Representatives shall not choose a President whenever the right of choice shall devolve upon them, before the fourth day of March next following, then the Vice-President shall act as President, as in the case of death or other constitutional disability of the President.

2. The person having the greatest number of votes as Vice-President, shall be the Vice-President, if such number be a majority of the whole number of Electors appointed, and if no person have a majority, then from the two highest numbers on the list, the Senate shall choose the Vice-President; a quorum for the purpose shall consist of two-thirds of the whole number of Senators, and a majority of the whole number shall be necessary to a choice.

3. But no person constitutionally ineligible to the office of President shall be eligible to that of Vice-President of the United States.

CONSTITUTION OF THE UNITED STATES,

WASHINGTON'S

FAREWELL ADDRESS,

AND

The Declaration of Independence.

Three very beautiful engravings on steel, commemorative of America's independence, of the Union, and of the retiring of General Washington from the Presidency, after victory to our arms had been secured, and peace again invited to the pursuits of commerce.

The DECLARATION is encircled by the Coat of Arms of the original thirteen States, with a fine illustration of

The National Washington Monument,

AND

THE MEMBERS OF THE CONTINENTAL CONGRESS SIGNING THE INSTRUMENT THE PLATE COMMEMORATES.

The Constitution by an emblematical border, representing Justice, the American Eagle, Commerce, Agriculture, and a view of the

BATTLE OF THE CONSTITUTION AND GUERRIERE.

The Address, by representations of important events in Washington's life—his Place of Birth, his Marriage, as a Farmer, the Field of Monmouth, Resigning his Commission, his Tomb, and a

Beautiful Portrait of Washington.

This set of prints is the most appropriate, and should find a place in the library, parlor, or drawing-room of every American, as the cost places them within the reach of all.

PRICE 50 CENTS EACH; or, $1 FOR THE THREE.

Size of Engraved Surface, 12x17 in.; printed on paper 15x23 in.

PUBLISHED BY
J. C. BUTTRE, 48 FRANKLIN STREET, NEW-YORK.

☞ Copies carefully mailed, free of postage, on receipt of price. Agents wanted to canvass and sell all over the United States.

PORTRAITS

OF

𝕻𝖗𝖊𝖘𝖎𝖉𝖊𝖓𝖙𝖎𝖆𝖑 𝕮𝖆𝖓𝖉𝖎𝖉𝖆𝖙𝖊𝖘,

BEAUTIFULLY ENGRAVED ON STEEL,

MOSTLY FROM

BRADY'S CELEBRATED PHOTOGRAPHS,

PRINTED ON PROOF PAPER, 11x15 INCHES.

SUITABLE FOR FRAMING OR PRESERVING IN PORTFOLIOS. THEY ARE RELIABLE FOR THEIR CORRECTNESS AND BEAUTY OF EXECUTION, AND CONSIST OF THE FOLLOWING, VIZ. :—

ABRAHAM LINCOLN, HANNIBAL HAMLIN.

JOHN BELL, EDWARD EVERETT.

STEPH. A. DOUGLAS, HERSCHEL V. JOHNSON.

JOHN C. BRECKINRIDGE, JOSEPH LANE.

PRICE 25 CENTS EACH.

A Copy of either portrait sent, free of postage, on receipt of the price.

Engraved and Published by J. C. BUTTRE,

48 FRANKLIN STREET, NEW-YORK.